CAREERS IN COMPUTER TECHNOLOGY™

CAREERS IN

Internet Security

DANIEL E. HARMON

ROSEN
PUBLISHING

Published in 2011 by The Rosen Publishing Group, Inc.
29 East 21st Street, New York, NY 10010

First Edition

Library of Congress Cataloging-in-Publication Data

Harmon, Daniel E.
Careers in Internet security / Daniel E. Harmon.
    p. cm.—(Careers in computer technology)
Includes bibliographical references and index.
ISBN 978-1-4488-1315-5 (library binding)
1. Internet—Vocational guidance—Juvenile literature. 2. Internet—
Security measures—Juvenile literature. I. Title.
TK5105.875.I57H362 2011
005.8—dc22

                                                    2010006860

Manufactured in the United States of America

CPSIA Compliance Information: Batch #W11YA: For further information, contact Rosen Publishing, New York, New York,
at 1-800-237-9932.

On the cover: The global scope of the Internet is what makes it such a
powerful platform for communications and information exchange. It also
means the Net poses worldwide security threats.

Contents

INTRODUCTION

Modern historians say the Internet has changed the course of history. Almost no one twenty or thirty years ago imagined what today's online lifestyle would be like. The Internet (or Net) has quietly revolutionized worldwide society.

The Internet has mushroomed into an enormous connected platform that is hard to define. Most people don't fully understand how big and powerful it is. It is a tremendous benefit to society. Through the Internet, computer users can find answers to nearly any question, usually in a matter of seconds or minutes. However, they can find themselves targets of evil forces in about the same amount of time. Although it is a great boon, the Net is a wide-open playground for individuals and organizations bent on mischief and crime.

The Internet has become powerful for two main purposes: information exchange and communications. The information explosion brought about by personal computers and the Internet holds great promise. People have very quick access to huge volumes of information that were unavailable not long ago. In addition, it is very easy to communicate with millions of people around the globe via e-mail and social networking services.

Most people in the United States, from small children to their great-grandparents, use computers and the Internet. But studies reveal that many users are careless, opening themselves to cyber attacks that range from annoying disruptions to devastating data thefts.

How do they protect themselves? Home users take care of their own security. The procedures are simple: Use a high-quality antivirus program, keep the virus definitions updated, and periodically scan the entire computer drive for infections. Meanwhile, avoid risky Web sites and activities and learn to recognize scams. (Don't open strange file attachments, click unknown hyperlinks, or respond to spammers whose offers seem too good to be true.)

Security is much more complicated for businesses, industries, government agencies, and other organizations. They rely heavily on computer technology. Business owners and agency administrators take precautions similar to those of home users, but on a larger scale. They, too, equip their computer systems with antivirus, antispyware, and firewall protection. But they must do more. They have wide networks of employees and outside contacts—thousands of people, in some situations. They store vast databases of information that might include millions of electronic documents. Many documents and e-mail records are private and sensitive. They must be guarded effectively because they are very attractive targets for information and identity thieves.

At this level, Internet security (also called cyber security) calls for much more than a $60 off-the-shelf utility program. It calls for a new class of security professional. Some large companies and organizations employ security professionals to work for them full-time. Others pay outside services to take care of security.

For young people who are interested in protecting Internet users from both accidental and deliberate dangers, the outlook is excellent. Career opportunities are numerous and increasing.

CHAPTER 1

The Need for Security on the Information Superhighway

Almost a hundred suspects in the United States and Egypt were arrested in October 2009 for participating in a major phishing expedition. Phishing is a type of Internet con. Victims are tricked into providing personal information to individuals or organizations they trust when, in fact, they're dealing with impostors. This phishing ring allegedly stole account information from hundreds, possibly thousands, of U.S. bank customers. The thieves made off with $1.5 million.

The two-year investigation was led by the Los Angeles office of the Federal Bureau of Investigation (FBI). Agents worked with the Secret Service and other law enforcement agencies in the United States and Egypt. The FBI wryly dubbed the takedown Operation Phish Phry.

Robert Mueller, FBI director, has called the struggle to secure the Internet a "cyber arms race." It pits law enforcers and information security professionals against super-intelligent hackers, crime syndicates, and terrorists. The frontier is expanding.

The 2009 Phish Phry was just one of a growing number of Internet crime cases. A few examples from past years include the following:

- In 2002, a disgruntled former employee of a New Jersey engineering corporation was convicted of

01000100101101101011010101110010010110010010101011010101010100010101101

FBI officials announce the arrest of scores of individuals in the United States and Egypt in October 2009. The suspects carried out a type of information theft scam called phishing.

installing a "time bomb" bug on the firm's computers. The malicious program permanently deleted the company's manufacturing software, costing at least $10 million in lost contracts and sales. The criminal was sentenced to forty-one months in prison.

• A former information technology (IT) officer for a Kazakhstan security company was sentenced to four years in prison in 2003. He schemed to steal confidential information from the computer system of a U.S. financial information company. He also threatened to publicize the breach unless the company paid him $200,000.

- A hacker was sentenced to nine years in prison in 2004 for trying to steal customer credit card information from a retail corporation's nationwide computer system. He and a partner cracked the wireless network of a retail store in Michigan. From there, they gained access to the company's central computer system in North Carolina.

- A California man in 2006 used a botnet program to infect computers at a Seattle hospital. The U.S. Department of Justice reported, "These disruptions affected the hospital's systems in numerous ways: doors to the operating rooms did not open, pagers did not work, and computers in the intensive care unit shut down." The hospital soon was able to restore order by resorting to its backup computer systems. The same intruder was responsible for more than $135,000 in damage to military computers in the United States and Germany.

Many cyber criminals, the U.S. Department of Justice notes, are juveniles. The first American juvenile sentenced to prison time (six months) was a sixteen-year-old from Miami, Florida, known as "c0mrade," who pleaded guilty in 2000 to hacking a military computer.

EXPLOITING SOCIETY'S NEW WAY OF LIFE

The Internet has become a modern necessity—and a tempting tool for crime. It provides a vehicle for instant, constant communication among friends, relatives, and business professionals. It offers a way to find and exchange enormous amounts of information very quickly. Google any term of interest, and a list of thousands of resources will likely appear in a matter of seconds.

Individuals and businesses use the Internet for two primary purposes: communication and information.

Texting and other forms of social networking—Facebook, Twitter, and MySpace, for example—are regular forms of communication for billions of people, especially teenagers.

Communication. Individuals frequently exchange text messages and e-mail. They post their up-to-the-minute doings and whereabouts on Facebook and other social networking sites, letting their friends (some of whom may not be so friendly) know all about their daily lives. They publish photos and videos of themselves and the things that interest them. They present very personal thoughts and details in their so-called digital diaries. Thanks to the Internet, they don't merely "talk" to one another; they continually communicate a depth of information about themselves to other people. Many parents are highly disturbed when they belatedly sign up for Facebook, MySpace, or YouTube and see some of the material their children have been posting for the world to see.

Businesses, organizations, and government agencies provide platforms for electronic communication among employees and supervisors, sales staff and customers, and people who work in related businesses. They, too, send out a bombardment of messages by e-mail. Organizations that sell products and services have also learned to use social networking platforms to communicate with new and potential buyers.

Information. Students go online to find material they need for homework and project assignments. Hobbyists log on to learn what they can about their special interests. Cooks look for recipes. Injury and disease victims look for advice to help them cope. Genealogists seek family connections and histories that go back hundreds of years. Writers and reporters find information about whatever topic they're covering.

Members of organizations, businesses, and agencies use the Internet to conduct research and obtain information from around the world. At the same time, the organization itself becomes an information source. It publishes—at its Web site, blog, or other Internet location—useful information for clients, customers, and curious visitors. This information may be in the form of articles, instruction booklets, or entire libraries of full-length books. The data collection might include pages of statistics, images, and audio/video presentations.

Internet users engage in a third purpose: entertainment. Online games and entertainment sites entice workers on the job as well as home computerists. Internet gaming systems and leisure Web sites have been favorite targets of cyber criminals for years.

WHAT ARE THE RISKS?

Computer viruses and worms are the most common threats. They can be transmitted through the simple exchange of files between coworkers and friends if one of the file sharers has an infected computer. They may be transmitted globally over the Internet.

Malicious viruses began to appear and increase in number in the late 1980s. A victim can be exposed simply by opening a computer file containing a virus program. It may cause only mischief—displaying an obscene image or message onscreen. It may cause tremendous hardship—slowing the computer's operation to a crawl over a period of days or weeks, deleting files and even destroying the operating system and wiping out the hard drive contents.

There are different types of viruses. An interesting example is a zombie. The hacker (or hacker organization) plants the program on thousands of computers. This program tells all the zombie computers to send data to a targeted computer system to overwhelm it. The target might be a company or agency the hacker considers an enemy. Owners of the zombie machines are unaware this is going on.

A worm is a type of virus that uses the Internet or a local network to spread itself. For instance, a worm may commandeer the address book on a computer and send a dangerous e-mail memo to all the recipients. This memo appears to come from the legitimate address book owner. The message may contain an interesting-looking file attachment or Web link. When a recipient clicks the attachment or the link, trouble follows.

An increasingly common cyber scam is phishing, demonstrated by the 2009 "Phish Phry" case. It takes advantage of the social nature of the Internet to lure unsuspecting Web surfers and e-mail users into traps. A phishing criminal may, for example, create a Web site that visually duplicates that of a bank or credit card company. The scammer then sends thousands or millions of e-mail messages, perhaps stating that the recipient's account has been temporarily suspended. To reactivate the account, the recipient is given a link to the card company or bank—which, in reality, takes the victim to the criminal's phony site. There, the victim is required to enter the account number and personal information. This provides the criminal with the details necessary to withdraw funds or make charges to the account.

Another example of phishing is the social networking scam known as the Koobface virus. A member of a network such as Facebook or MySpace may log on one day and see a post from someone who appears to be a friend. The message says something to this effect: "What a sexy video of you! Did you really post this?!?" Or "Wow! I've never seen you in THAT outfit!!!" Below the teaser is a link. Instinctively, the startled victim clicks the link to see what reputation-ruining item someone has spread all around the world. This brings a pop-up message informing the visitor that to view the image or video, the latest version of a certain media player must be downloaded and installed. When the person clicks to download said program . . . malware awaits. (No risqué photo or video of the victim ever existed.)

Viruses, worms, and phishing scams are not the only kinds of invading malware that can cause problems to individuals as well as to office-wide computer systems. Spyware is employed by Internet advertisers. It is a utility program that installs itself on a user's computer hard drive while the user is visiting a Web site. Behind the scenes, it begins to report to the advertiser all the places the user goes on the Internet. This information helps the advertiser identify the user's personal interests. Advertisers sometimes share this data with other advertisers.

A more recent cyber crime device is ransomware. Criminals invade a personal computer online and encrypt the user's files, locking the victim out of his or her own data. To retrieve the files, the victim must pay a "ransom" to the file-jacker.

Threats are so varied that no single security program can tackle them all.

WHY DO HACKERS HACK?

Ron White, author of *How Computers Work*, says there are computer "hackers" and computer "crackers." There is a clear distinction. He writes that "most computer crackers are grossly egotistical." Their invasions via the Internet are more of a prank nature than an attempted data theft.

WHO PAYS FOR THE LOSSES?

Individuals who become victims of cyber crimes suffer personal consequences. These include the loss of money, loss of privacy, public humiliation, and damage to their computers. Problems may take hours or days to correct—if they can be corrected.

When banks and other companies and agencies lose sensitive information about their clients, customers, and employees, they may face lawsuits. It's their responsibility to secure the information. In many suits, individuals have won heavy settlements or judgments by successfully arguing that the company failed to provide adequate security.

In an interesting twist, a Texas bank in November 2009 sued one of its corporate customers after cyber criminals in Europe stole $800,000 from the customer's account. The bank recovered most of the money, but the corporation demanded that the bank repay the rest. The company claimed the bank's security was inadequate. The bank, on the other hand, filed a suit asking a U.S. district court to confirm that its security was not at fault. According to the suit, the criminals obtained the account access information from the company—not from the bank.

Disruptive and disgusting as they are, they usually don't cause lasting, irreversible damage. They want attention. "They can't resist leaving a program or note that's a digital sign of Zorro, something to let you know that while you might own the computer, the cracker owns its soul."

Criminal hackers are after much more. They want to either steal valuable information from a victim's computer or

Office supply and department stores carry choices of anti-malware software suites. If they investigate carefully, consumers can also find and download free security programs from the Internet.

network, or wreck the victim's computer operations. Hacker attacks have forced businesses to close. They have resulted in multimillion-dollar lawsuits, and they have shaken the public's confidence in government and banking institutions.

FBI director Mueller says cyber crimes may be far more devious than they appear on the surface. "Something that looks like an ordinary phishing scam may be an attempt by a terrorist group to raise funding for an organization."

White observes, "Fortunately, while no system, from a home PC to an Internet-connected corporate supercomputer, is totally crack-proof, as a user there are tools at your disposal that can help you keep control of your PC." Antivirus programs, firewalls, and complex, frequently changed passwords are the most often-employed examples.

THE NEED FOR SECURITY SPECIALISTS

Individual computer users are expected to take care of their own security. They can resolve problems by guarding their PCs with up-to-date anti-malware programs. They should be aware of the Internet's dangers and adopt commonsense habits. Individuals' security headaches might be termed Internet security skirmishes.

The scarier concern by far is cyber criminals' bombardment of large computer systems, especially those used by government and financial institutions. Ordinary antivirus software, firewalls, password protection, and data encryption programs may not suffice. This is the war zone of Internet security, where highly skilled professional defenders are in great demand.

Financial company and government computers have been prime victims of hackers since the early years of Internet history, but they aren't the only targets. In November 2009, the FBI warned of "noticeable increases" in hacking attempts against law firm computer systems. SecureWorks, a security firm based in Atlanta, Georgia, in January 2010 reported that health care organizations are also under accelerated attacks. The firm reported more than thirteen thousand health care data attacks in the last quarter of 2009. That was more than twice the combined number during the first three quarters.

Banks, credit card companies, and other institutions electronically transmit and store private customer data. They hire experts to protect their customers' account information, Social Security numbers, driver's license numbers, etc. Insurance companies, law firms, hospitals, libraries, government agencies, and other entities that rely on the Internet must likewise ensure data security. While guarding against threats from the outside, they must guard against carelessness and abuse on the inside. They need knowledgeable information managers to monitor the computer use of their staff. Employees who engage in social networking, shopping, and Web browsing while at work pose risks to their employers. Their activities could lose confidential customer information and their employers' business and trade secrets.

Simon Willison, a noted Web developer, writer, and speaker, cautions, "Keeping your Web application secure is an ongoing process—new classes of vulnerabilities are discovered with surprising frequency, and if you don't keep on top of them, you could be in for a nasty surprise."

Gavin Bell, author of *Building Social Web Applications*, says, "Security is hard to do well; most frameworks and tools are set up to make things easy to hook up and implement, with security left as an afterthought." He also notes that site security is "painstaking work." Nonetheless, Bell advises, "It would be wise to make sure that your entire development team has a good understanding of the current security threats that exist on the Web."

Companies, organizations, and government agencies are taking heed. That is why the services of Internet security experts are always in demand.

CHAPTER ②

Types of Internet Security Professionals

Teams of computer science students at six higher learning institutions in 2009 trained for six months in an intense new form of "ninja" defense. Their task was to learn how to defend business computer networks from hacker attacks. After a two-day competition, the team from California State Polytechnic University in Pomona triumphed.

It was more than an academic award for the students. The giant aerospace company Boeing offered all of them jobs. It indicated the urgent demand for smart computer science graduates in the field of Internet security. As security threats mount, so do efforts to thwart e-criminals. Companies and government agencies are willing to pay well for "cyber ninjas."

THE NEW GUARDIANS OF COMMUNICATIONS AND INFORMATION

Internet security professionals generally belong to the category of workers the Bureau of Labor Statistics' *Occupational Outlook Handbook* calls "computer specialists." Specialists represent more than half of the job force involved in computer systems design and maintenance. Some specialists develop computer software. Some design complete information systems from scratch. Others—in escalating numbers—are responsible for handling network security.

Most of these professionals work, either directly or indirectly, in an area of computerization known as IT—information technology. Information technology workers deal with different aspects of the electronic information that is collected and used by individuals, companies, organizations, and government agencies. The use of electronic data regularly involves the Internet.

A network administrator for an online storage company tests the security of a client's data center. Security professionals look for weaknesses in their customers' systems that can result in data theft.

Some IT professionals are dedicated to making sure the people who employ them can find the information they need, completely and quickly. Their job is to store, manage, and maintain data collections. Other professionals do not view the collected information in the same way as data managers and end users. They focus on the highly technical computer platforms that process the information. In both types of jobs, though, security is a concern. Cyber criminals target electronic information, and they get to it through the software and systems that process it.

The *Occupational Outlook Handbook* describes professions in computer systems design and related services. Systems developers create software (computer programs) for specific hardware (the machines that run the programs). Their goal is to provide the most effective way for end users (nontechnical computerists in all walks of life) to obtain the information they want. End users must be able to communicate and exchange this information electronically. They do so via either the Internet or a company extranet (which may be linked to the Internet).

Many large corporations and government departments have their own systems design staff. Others engage outside services to develop the system, install it, and train the staff. Thus, a professional in these areas might work for a large company or government agency, or for a computer-related service.

In most situations, the security professional's workplace is in a comfortable, indoor office. Some days are routine. Others bring frenzied activity and high stress. Travel may be required to the locations of distant clients and problem sites.

CAREERS IN COMPUTER *SYSTEMS DESIGN AND RELATED SERVICES*

In most roles, Internet security specialists must know computer software and systems from the inside out. They need to understand what kinds of programming and design weaknesses leave a system or network vulnerable to attack from the Internet. Many security professionals are trained and experienced programmers and systems designers. Although they were not trained initially as security professionals, they understand security issues.

Computer software programmers are hired by businesses, industries, large organizations, government agencies, and outside service companies. They write and test the software programs that operate their clients' information and communication systems.

Programmers are usually supervised by software engineers or systems analysts. The analysts determine what the software and the entire system need to accomplish. The programmers write the code—the logical set of instructions that operate the computer—that will achieve those objectives. Most code is written in a very sophisticated programming language: C++, Java, Python, etc.

Programmers are not necessarily Internet security specialists. They must be aware, however, of security threats that can infect their programming code. Security specialists, meanwhile, must understand the sections of programming code that might be vulnerable to attack. New threats loom, with hackers constantly experimenting to find ways to overcome programs and systems.

```
va.io.*;
va.net.*;
va.security.*;

otection;

lass Client {
    void sendAuthenticatio
utStream outStream) thr
outputStream out = new
    t1 = (new Date()).ge
le q1 = Math.random()
[] protected1 = Prot
    t2 = (new Date()).
le q2 = Math.random
[] protected2 = Pr
writeUTF(user);
writeInt(protecte
write(protected2)
flush();

tatic void
```

Computer program code is a wilderness of meaningless lines to most people. A computer programmer, though, can read and write it as easily as a letter or e-memo.

At a higher level, computer software engineers are skilled programmers, but they usually leave the actual programming to others. Engineers design programs and applications to meet a client's specific needs and solve specific problems. During and after the programming process, they test and evaluate the programmers' work.

The role of computer systems analysts and testers is to make sure software and hardware are implemented and work together efficiently. They work with programmers and engineers during the development process and with managers afterward. Some analysts and testers are employed by the government to test and approve Internet security systems that are developed by outside contractors.

Network systems and data communications analysts are professionals who plan, design, test, and evaluate networks. Network systems include local area networks (LANs—computers networked within an office), wide area networks (WANs—a system of connected LANs), Internet network systems, and intranets (Internet-like networks developed for use within a company or agency). The *Occupational Outlook Handbook* observes, "With the explosive growth of the Internet, this worker group has come to include a variety of occupations related to design, development, and maintenance of Web sites and their servers." For example, Web developers design and create Web sites. Webmasters then operate the sites, making sure they function as intended and contain only content that is approved by the site owners.

Support specialists are technical specialists who identify and resolve problems. They also help maintain their employers' computer systems by regularly running diagnostic utilities, backing up data, operating telephone help desks, etc.

SECURITY WORK CAN LEAD TO HIGH DRAMA

Computer security projects and hacker investigations sometimes involve professionals in international intrigue. Law enforcement officers and prosecutors in several countries combined forces to break up a massive credit card theft operation in November 2009. Hackers from Estonia, Russia, and Moldova were charged with wire fraud, conspiracy, identity theft, and related crimes in the theft of account numbers from a credit card processing company in Atlanta, Georgia.

According to the U.S. Department of Justice (DOJ), the defendants "used sophisticated hacking techniques" to break through the protection of customers' payroll debit cards. Some companies let employees draw their pay from ATMs, using their debit cards. In this case, the hackers created false debit cards to steal more than $9 million from more than two thousand ATMs in some three hundred cities around the world. The theft, which was carried out in less than twelve hours, was "perhaps the most sophisticated and organized computer fraud attack ever conducted," a DOJ official said.

The DOJ said police and prosecutors in the United States, Estonia, Hong Kong, and the Netherlands cooperated in breaking the ring.

Computer and information systems managers oversee the work of others on the IT team, including programmers and systems analysts. In fact, they decide which types of professionals need to be on the team and how many. They determine what equipment is required to get the job done. They coordinate the team's activities, from program and systems design, to hardware and software installation, to the development and construction of computer networks and Internet sites.

RELATED OCCUPATIONS

Internet security professionals are called on to perform many tasks. If hired by an organization or company, they may be responsible for controlling and monitoring workers' access to company files and the Internet and for managing employees' log-on accounts and passwords. They see that file encryption methods are effective. They make sure former employees no longer have access to the files—or access to the Internet through the company's computer system. Toby Skandier, in his book *Network Administrator Street Smarts*, describes sample tasks, how professionals carry them out step-by-step, and how long the tasks will likely take.

Some security experts cope with threats not only from the Internet but also from within smaller networks. Many companies, agencies, and large professional firms develop what might be called "mini" Internets. They need specialists to create, manage, and secure them.

Information technology author C. J. Rhoads defines these networks: "An intranet is when we use Internet technologies . . . to provide our own employees with access to needed information . . . An extranet allows us to utilize the power of the public Internet for a select group of people—a company's sales force, representatives, or partners."

Countless organizations have large databases of sensitive customer and client information. They keep this information in electronic systems that use—and rely on—the Internet. These organizations include financial institutions, retail store chains and product vendors that offer online shopping, online auction platforms, and associations that allow their members to pay dues online. Such institutions find themselves under assault by hackers. They need highly skilled electronic security workers.

A fairly recent area of security concern is "in the cloud." In cloud computing, companies, agencies, and individuals pay an Internet service provider to let them use programs online (programs that are not installed on their own computers). The cloud service may also store customers' files and manage access to those files. Huge volumes of information can be housed and used online—in the Internet "cloud." Neal Weinberg, a writer for *Network World*, points to two well-known examples of cloud computing platforms: Amazon and Google, "both of which basically rent their data-center

Director Mark Sullivan of the Secret Service (left) and Attorney General Michael Mukasey appear at a 2008 news conference announcing the breakup of a retail hacking ring.

resources to outside customers." Cloud services hire security experts to guarantee that their customers' information and online operations are secure.

Contractors for federal, state, or local governments also need data security professionals. Thousands of companies supply government agencies with services, systems, and equipment. They must be able to guarantee that the secrets and methods of operation they furnish the government with are not breached by Internet hackers. Many firms, particularly those under contract with the military, hire software programmers to write security programs.

Some security professionals work as consultants, either to the government and industry sectors or to companies that consult with those entities. Consultants may work solo or for (or start their own) consulting firms. Some firms offer a team of advisers who are experienced in different areas of information management and security.

The government itself employs technology specialists who thoroughly understand security science. They test the programs of their contracting companies to make sure they meet government security standards and are effective against hackers.

At or near the forefront of Internet security personnel employers are computer companies and Internet-based operators. Microsoft, the software supergiant, has been the primary object of hackers for many years. More recently, Adobe Systems has come under repeated attack. Hundreds of millions of people use Adobe Acrobat, Reader, Flash Player, and other popular programs. In 2009, hackers aggressively looked for weaknesses in Reader and Flash Player that would give them access to the computers of poorly protected end users. As a result, the company stepped up its security efforts.

Such companies employ whole staffs of Internet security experts. So do e-mail, social networking, and blog platforms that must keep their users' personal information private.

GOOD HACKERS

"Good" hackers accomplish several objectives in the fight against Internet crime. Some monitor clients' computer systems, constantly looking for potential weaknesses and blocking or disarming threats before damage occurs. This work occurs behind the scenes. The employer often does not realize, until later, that the security expert has engaged in battle and won.

Some companies and agencies periodically have their entire IT teams conduct a security audit. They put themselves

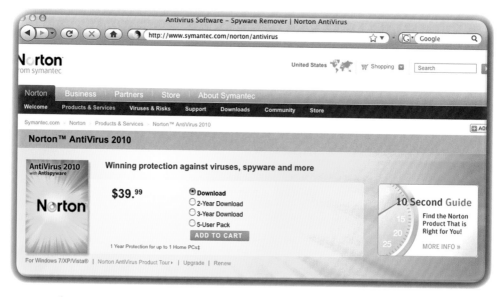

Software programs are available to help end users ward off computer viruses, spam, spyware, and other threats. The companies that market them employ "good" hackers to outwit the "bad" hackers.

in "bad guy" mode and scrutinize their systems from the viewpoint of an outside hacker trying to break in. They identify possible weaknesses and remedy them.

Other good hackers devote their talents to developing cures to new viruses. Security suite makers such as Symantec, Kaspersky, Panda, iolo technologies, McAfee, and Webroot guard against millions of computer viruses and develop antidotes to hundreds of new bugs each week. They know they must keep their customers' machines as up-to-date with protection as possible.

Security experts design other kinds of programs that protect computer systems from hacking, such as OAuth. OAuth is an Internet protocol, or programming system. It was developed to let people share contact lists, photos, and other personal information among different Web sites without risking the theft of their user names and passwords.

Still others work for law enforcement agencies to trap or track down cyber criminals.

SECURE DATA RECOVERY AND DISCOVERY

Another related profession is in electronic data recovery. Using special software tools and hardware expertise, recovery specialists repair the damage from a computer disaster, whether caused by accident or hacker attack. They restore a company's or agency's electronic information so that normal operations can resume. They also work with their clients in advance, inspecting and monitoring their systems. These experts can point out vulnerabilities to Internet attacks and suggest preventive and backup strategies.

In the legal area, Internet issues of growing concern relate to electronic data discovery (EDD). When lawsuits are filed, lawyers and firms are required to provide opposing parties with electronic records. These records include e-mail that might be of interest in the case. EDD professionals on all sides, working closely with information technology departments, are security minded. They must ensure that electronic records are delivered, received, and processed without risk of loss to any of the parties involved. In large cases, thousands of individuals may be affected. This kind of sensitive data exchange has become more complicated with the transfer of files in international, or cross-border, electronic discovery. Various countries have different legal procedures and laws governing information exchange.

All Internet security professionals must stay abreast of the latest local and national laws and industry regulations concerning data security. Laws affect not just EDD in lawsuits but also the whole range of Internet concerns, including those associated with social networking. Mark Weatherford, the state of California's chief information security officer, observes, "Because social media is all about the weakest link and hardest-to-control aspect of the security chain (people), phishing and the growing array of tactics cyber criminals use to exploit, dupe, and deceive will continue to expand." Weatherford predicts "a vast increase in the number of incidents related to loss of Personally Identifiable Information (PII) and consequently, new and more regulations for both business and government to protect PII and other sensitive data."

CHAPTER 3

Teenagers can find cyber security to be an exciting challenge. They are especially equipped for Internet-related careers because they know the Internet. They regularly use computers and go online. Most are engaged in texting, chatting, blogging, and virtual gaming. Many take digital photos and record videos and share them with friends. Some have created elaborate Web sites.

Career advisers point to a growing need for Internet security professionals. They worry, however, that many talented and Internet-savvy students are uninterested in two subjects that are vital to pursuing a technology career: math and science. In other words, these young people revel in the fun of the Internet but not in the nitty-gritty of what makes the Net work . . . and what makes it dangerous.

At the basic level, security specialists need a thorough understanding not just of the Internet but also of office computer networks and intranets. They must be familiar with the fundamental aspects of Internet use: Web navigation, Web site design and programming, data downloading and uploading, file exchanging, communication via single and massive e-mail transmittals, the invasion of computers by adware and spyware, the values and dangers of electronic links, the workings of social network platforms, the uses of media players and digital image managers, and much more.

From there, it gets more complicated. Details are explained in the chapters on training and careers.

EARN WHILE YOU LEARN AS AN AFTER-SCHOOL GEEK

American teenagers and young adults are recognized as being keenly knowledgeable about technology—especially about the Internet, smartphones and other mobile devices, and applications. Many business professionals have little time to experiment with technology, but they need to take advantage of it. They may be willing to pay students for their services.

High school students have found after-school and weekend computer work at retail stores, law offices, charitable organizations, and various other workplaces. They set up new hardware and install software, conduct regular system backups and anti-malware scans, solve computer problems, create Web sites, and launch and maintain blogs. Their tasks may require only an hour or two each week, or may become regular part-time jobs. Pay in many cases exceeds minimum wage. A greater benefit is the early experience they gain in dealing with real-world computer and Internet issues—which looks very good on an employment résumé.

PERSONALITY TRAITS AND INTEREST AREAS

The *Occupational Outlook Handbook* notes that people interested in this type of career will need, in addition to an academic degree, "significant hands-on experience with computers.

A person interested in an Internet security career obviously must be thoroughly familiar with computing in general and the Net in particular. For today's teenagers, this requirement is an advantage.

They also must possess strong problem-solving, analytical, and communication skills because troubleshooting and helping others are their main job functions."

More insight can be gleaned from some of the job postings by companies that employ specialists in computerization and related fields. VeriSign (http://www.verisign.com), for instance, is a well-known company that protects companies' online transactions and private information. It registers domain names and guards Internet business activities with data encryption, digital ID authentication or verification, and other services. VeriSign is one of thousands of technology companies that are interested in the talents of Internet security specialists. In many of its job announcements, it describes the basic skill set it looks for, in addition to the applicant's education and experience. Here are several examples:

Senior Cyber Security Intelligence Analyst. "Candidates must possess outstanding written and oral communication skills and have the ability to prioritize work." They must be able to work with a team or independently. They should be gifted problem solvers, as the *Occupational Outlook Handbook* notes—and they should bring "originality and creativity" to problem solving.

By the time they're ready to apply for such a job, applicants will have excellent computer skills. They also will have, in VeriSign's description, "in-depth knowledge of the security concerns facing large enterprises and government agencies; familiarity with cyber threats, defenses, motivations and techniques; familiarity with intelligence analysis tools, methods, and the intelligence life cycle; ability to write analytical information products; ability to prepare and present research findings in both client and public settings; experience distilling raw information into actionable intelligence; ability to maintain or develop professional contacts in the cyber security community and in client industries, including finance and government."

Intelligence Analyst III. Here, the applicant needs what VeriSign calls "an uncommon blend of technical knowledge and a strong understanding of business operations." That's because analysts in this area must "understand how the technical dimension of threats may impact the organization's functions."

The analyst must be familiar with the vulnerabilities of IT systems, hacker techniques, malicious software code, and criminal behavior. Such other subjects as social science, business management evaluation methods, and statistics are important. Intelligence analysts are advanced users of the Internet for research. They are especially familiar with sources related to information security.

Again, problem-solving skills are a must. So are skills in communicating with others, data analysis, and "abstract processes." This professional has technical knowledge in advanced programs, programming languages, networks, and Web servers. The analyst also knows general office applications (word processors, spreadsheets, Web browsers, etc.).

The analyst should have a working knowledge of the way financial companies operate—not only in the United States but also abroad. Much of the information at stake is confidential. That means the analyst must know the local regulations concerning the handling of sensitive information. The person has to be able to work alone or with a team and to function well under pressure. Besides English, the worker may need to be proficient in German, French, and/or another European language.

VeriSign added an interesting required characteristic to this job listing: "Learns from mistakes or successes for future planning and development."

Network Engineer. A candidate for this kind of job must have complex technical engineering training and experience, especially in terms of international networking issues. VeriSign also described personal traits: "The individual should be highly motivated, results-oriented, and should have excellent communication, writing, presentation, and troubleshooting skills. The candidate should have experience interacting with management on complex technical issues." Also required is a "balance" of skills in problem solving, hands-on analysis, and documentation drafting.

Engineer IV. This advanced level of engineer has to be an expert in software development, engineering, tools, and processes, but also needs a special set of strong personal skills. Those skills include the ability to communicate with engineers at different levels and to communicate verbally, in writing, and through presentations. The company wants a self-starter requiring little supervision.

More is required: good skills in planning and organizing and in troubleshooting and problem solving. The engineer must be able to work alone or as a team member and must have experience as a technical project leader.

Computer security analysts and engineers should be able to work alone and in teams. They are often called on to make presentations and to communicate with client company officials.

THERE IS PLENTY OF TIME TO LEARN

Many high school students will shake their heads at some of the skills noted above. They shouldn't. Those are not skill sets expected of teenagers who aspire to technology careers. They are skills that eventually will be acquired. Students should be willing to pursue them and must possess basic interests in technology—notably, troubleshooting. They will gain the other skills in time.

Eventually, Internet security professionals have to learn about things that do not relate directly to the Internet. For example, they need to know what Net security has to do with tasks like marketing, future planning, business tax calculations, and handling employee payrolls. They must understand the connections between the company or agency that employs them and the employer's customers or members—and how the Internet can affect those local connections.

High school students do not have to keep up with the latest regulations and court rulings that affect the Internet. If they become Net security professionals, though, they will have to understand what federal and state laws allow and what they forbid. In the process of defeating cyber lawbreakers, they must be sure they and their employers do not run afoul of the law themselves. Laws and regulations involve every area of Internet use from consumer privacy to advertising and marketing.

Internet security covers a wide spectrum of concerns and issues. A career in this area will require substantial training.

CHAPTER 4
Required Training

Polytechnic universities and colleges around the United States are creating new programs in Internet security. They recognize that they are not graduating enough trained security professionals to meet the mushrooming demands of government, military, technology, and business employers.

A number of institutions around the country already have established curricula in computer science fields related to Net security. Newer programs include degrees in cyber security and information security. Some are offered online.

In recent years, higher learning institutions have begun offering degrees in different subjects related directly to Internet security. Online programs provide further educational options.

Most computer-related jobs require advanced levels of technology training. Programmers and software engineers usually hold at least a bachelor's degree in computer science, mathematics, or information management. Many have earned master's degrees.

Employers' needs will determine the education and training levels expected of prospective employees. The *Occupational Outlook Handbook* notes that "the recent emphasis on information security has increased the demand for workers with expertise in security services. Employers also are demanding workers with skill and expertise in other fields."

TRAINING FOR CAREERS IN COMPUTER SYSTEMS DESIGN AND RELATED SERVICES

Different computer jobs have different training requirements. Most degree programs have certain subjects in common, however—most notably, science and math.

There are "no universal educational requirements" for computer software programmers, the *Occupational Outlook Handbook* observes. For other jobs, a two-year degree or computer-related certificate will suffice "as long as applicants possess the right technical skills." For some roles, the worker must have a technical or professional certificate. The handbook notes that "many organizations now assist employees in becoming certified."

During the early years of computing in the mid-twentieth century, many of the best programmers learned what they needed to know either on the job or on their own (or both).

Even today, some programmers do not hold college degrees. However, post–high school education has become practically mandatory for newcomers to this type of job for two reasons. First, computer security work has become more complicated. Second, the job market is now filled with applicants who hold undergraduate and advanced degrees in computer science, math, or information technology. Some programmers today hold physical science degrees and have taken extra courses in computer programming.

For computer software engineers, a bachelor's degree or higher will be required. The *Occupational Outlook Handbook* states that they also need "broad knowledge and experience with computer systems and technologies." Applications software engineers typically graduate from programs that concentrate in computer science and software engineering. Systems software engineers usually major in computer science or information systems. "Graduate degrees are preferred for some of the more complex software engineering jobs," the handbook points out. "Computer software engineers may also benefit from getting a technical or professional certification."

Systems analysts and testers hold a variety of jobs. Webmasters and network or communications analysts may only need an associate's degree or certificate in a related field. A bachelor's degree in either computer or information science or in management information systems is required for more advanced jobs. A master's degree in business administration, concentrating in information systems, may be required.

Most analysts have become specialists, and many hold more than one degree, plus certificates. The *Occupational Outlook Handbook* notes that certification in information security is especially needed for jobs in government agencies and academic institutions. This illustrates "the importance of keeping complex computer networks and vital electronic infrastructure safe from intruders."

Computer support specialists usually have at least an associate's degree in an area of technology. They also have years of experience working with computers and software. As technology advances, support specialists will need to learn new skills and acquire additional certification. Technology is one field in which the old saying particularly applies: "Education never ends."

Computer and information systems managers in most positions have at least a computer-related bachelor's degree. Some employers want managers who have earned an MBA (master's of business administration) or other graduate degree.

Most consultants to government agencies and corporations must have extensive technology experience. However, computer consulting firms may hire recent college graduates in computer-related majors and train them on the job.

EXAMPLES OF SPECIFIC JOBS AND REQUIREMENTS

This sampling of recent job openings posted by VeriSign, the data encryption and ID authentication specialist service, provides details of the kinds of qualifications employers seek in Net security personnel:

Senior Cyber Security Intelligence Analyst. This person, a member of a VeriSign security intelligence team, would

Workers in the Threat Operations Center of the National Security Agency monitor potential Internet security threats and issue alerts to the public, financial sectors, and other possible targets.

be "charged with directing the intelligence process and developing a common picture of the cyber security threat environment." Responsibilities would include "identifying and analyzing security incidents to assess severity and identify responsible parties."

This job required a bachelor's of science (BS) degree in computer or information science or information management "or other relevant security field." It also required extensive experience: more than five years in "an intelligence operation (cyber security or military intelligence operations preferred)"; more than two years working in a security operations center or with a computer emergency response team, or comparable cyber security experience; and more than three years making analytical reports. Candidates would be expected to know how to treat sensitive information. Travel could be involved up to 10 percent of the time.

Those were the *requirements*. Additional education and experience were *desired*: a master's of science (MS) degree, rather than a BS; military or business intelligence operational experience; an understanding of the way military, law enforcement, or intelligence agencies operate; and the "ability to implement technology tools, including customization and development of beta tools."

Intelligence Analyst III. Also called a threat intelligence analyst, this professional, based in the United Kingdom, would "work primarily on-site with the threat intelligence team of a major global bank." The expert would have a finger on the

An advanced criminal justice class studies the investigation of cold case files. Criminal justice and criminology are among the college curricula that could lead to an Internet security career.

pulse of the "cyber threat environments" of different countries, especially threats aimed at financial targets. The analyst would assess threats so that the bank's own security staff could respond accordingly. VeriSign estimated the individual would devote two-thirds of the time to threat analysis and the rest to helping the client organization reduce risks by providing security tools and guidance.

A bachelor's degree was required (master's preferred) in information security, economics, sociology, criminology, political science, computer science, or systems analysis. A business administration degree would be considered "if complemented with proper experience and secondary study." Ideally, applicants would have at least two years of experience in information security and a year of experience in finance. Travel within the United Kingdom and to the United States and Europe would be involved.

Network Engineer. A member of the shared networks team, this person would collaborate with different operations and design groups "to define standards and best practices, redesign and re-engineer network components when needed, and will participate in a 24x7 on-call rotation for trouble resolution." The candidate would also help detect and reduce security breaches.

The job required a bachelor's or master's degree in computer science or an equivalent education, plus network engineering experience with a commercial Internet service provider (ISP). VeriSign preferred a candidate with more than seven years of experience working with large networks. Applicants should be well-versed in Internet routing and networking protocols, firewalls, and related technologies. Advanced programming languages and system administration experience were assumed.

Engineer IV. Advanced engineering roles such as this require more experience than that for lower-level engineers. Here, system design and development duties were fast-paced with "aggressive schedules," calling for a "hands-on engineer with strong development skills." An interesting additional requirement was to be able to work with "minimal product requirement specifications" and "come up with requirements based on customer interactions."

The job required a bachelor's or master's degree in computer science or a related field with lengthy experience—at least eight years designing and developing software applications, at least five years of Java coding experience in Linux or Unix, and familiarity with numerous development programs and Web 2.0 concepts.

LEARNING OPPORTUNITIES ONLINE

A computer search will lead interested students to colleges and universities that offer degrees and classes in Internet security and related subjects. More and more higher learning institutions are developing security curricula each year as the demand for trained Net security professionals grows.

Some courses are available online. High school students may want to look into the offerings of such organizations as the SANS Technology Institute (http://www.sans.org) and the International Information Systems Security Certification Consortium, Inc. (ISC^2 [http://www.isc2.org]). The SANS Technology Institute in Bethesda, Maryland, offers training in computer security, information security, IT security, and network security. It provides both onsite and online instruction. The institute awards MS degrees in information security management and information security engineering.

TWO GRADUATE DEGREE PROGRAMS IN INFORMATION SECURITY

Among the newer master's degree programs in cyber security is the one offered online by Georgia Tech's College of Computing. The program is designed for professionals who already work in an area of information security and want to further their careers.

Master's candidates in the Georgia Tech program must complete courses in information security, cryptography, network security, secure computer systems, and security policies and strategies. They study the security of operating systems and computer applications. They also examine related subjects such as the IT routines of organizations and security issues involving industry and government.

Virginia College, which has campuses in six states and specializes in online training, offers an MS degree in cyber security. Courses include cyber law and research, cyber terrorism, viral activity and malware, math for security professionals, psychological profiling, cryptography, firewalls and other protective tools, intrusion detection systems, computer forensics, transmission security, and the handling of electronic data and government compliance.

The ISC² has offices in Vienna, Virginia, and abroad. The nonprofit organization offers various training and certification programs for security professionals.

TIP FOR TEENS: BEGIN AN APPLIED SELF-STUDY IN COMPUTING

Teenagers who are interested in Internet security careers can begin their initial preparation while in grade school. Many schools, including elementary schools, offer Internet- and computer-related clubs. Club members should learn as much as they can about the powers—and risks—of computers, smartphones, and online activities.

On their own, they should commit time to learning everything they can about the computers and software they use at home. They can also explore the Internet more broadly—not just the fun stuff (games and social networking) but serious issues as well.

A good way for teens to begin their study is by reading one or more of the introductory guidebooks that explain viruses, spyware, spam, and other Internet threats. They also should read basic books on how computers work. Pay attention to what may cause problems in everyday computing. What's happening during the boot-up process, during the minutes just after they turn on the machine? Why does the Windows operating interface seem fraught with delays? Why do e-mail checks and other online tasks sometimes slow the computer's performance to a crawl? How does a hard drive store information? Why should they bother to run defragmentation and cleanup utilities? Why doesn't simply deleting a file or e-mail message completely delete the item? How can "lost" files be recovered?

More to the point, security-minded young people should recognize the importance of anti-malware programs and learn how to make them function as effectively as possible to protect their computers. They should familiarize themselves with troubleshooting, diagnostic, and maintenance utilities.

They can explore YouTube, Facebook, Twitter, MySpace, blogs, Flickr, and other social networking platforms—and see what problems have been reported by users. They should learn about common malware intruders like Koobface and how they cleverly draw innocent Internet users into their schemes.

Budding technologists can learn how to create and maintain Web sites, not just with automated Web page creation programs but also with HTML and other programming codes. They can discover the usefulness of metatags and observe the ways in which metadata can be misused.

They should also consider the issues involved in wireless computing with laptop PCs and smartphones. Is the network they use at risk? What are some of the bad things that can happen to them while they are e-communicating? If their iPhone or BlackBerry is lost or stolen, can they be sure their personal information is locked?

The more ambitious aspiring security pros will learn something about the risks encountered by corporate and government Internet users. Terms like "private key" and "public key" encryption, "digital signatures," and "hash values" will become familiar to them.

Before they enter a post–high school program in computer science or security, high school students should learn as much as they can, on their own, about computers and the Internet.

CHAPTER 5

Launching a Career and Advancing in Internet Security

By the time they complete a college program in computer science or a related field, many budding Internet security workers have a good idea of who they want to work for and what they want to do. Others are unsure.

They should consider the different types of employers: government agencies, companies in many different branches of the computer industry, and businesses and professional service firms that need secure information technology. They should also look at consulting firms that contract with those employers to furnish outside security services.

JOBS IN GOVERNMENT

Military and other government jobs in Internet security are on the rise. Security experts say the United States and other nations should expect "acts of cyberwar," the IDG News Service reported in January 2010. Such acts may include disrupting enemy communications—which the United States has already done in Iraq. As governments worldwide scramble for advantages in cyberspace, the United States must be prepared to respond to similar threats against it.

Authorities already know most Internet attacks originate in foreign countries. Pinpointing the exact sources, though, is difficult. Companies and agencies that have been attacked

The National Security Agency is a federal organization devoted to protecting the country from all threats, including those involving technology and the Internet.

have identified the hackers in only about a fourth of the episodes.

The U.S. Department of Homeland Security is one of several federal agencies likely to be hiring more cyber crime specialists in coming years. In its careers section (http://www.dhs.gov/xabout/careers), the department provides guidance for career seekers at every stage—entry-level, experienced professional, and retirees looking for part-time or short-term contractual work. It also features a section for young people, describing possible internships, training programs, and scholarships "to expose talented students to our broad national security mission."

Of special interest to career-minded students is the Department of Homeland Security's National Cyber Security Division (NCSD). The operational branch of the NCSD is the U.S. Computer Emergency Readiness Team (US-CERT). US-CERT focuses on defending the federal government against cyber attacks. It partners and shares information with many public and private security organizations. It also manages the National Cyber Alert System, which it defines as "America's first cohesive national cyber security system for identifying, analyzing, and prioritizing emerging vulnerabilities and threats."

Government agencies hire security specialists trained in subjects other than computer science. Legal professionals, for example, are needed to work with Internet security teams. The U.S. Department of Justice includes a Computer Crime and Intellectual Property Section (CCIPS). Its responsibility is "implementing the Department's national strategies in combating computer and intellectual property crimes worldwide. The Computer Crime Initiative is a comprehensive program designed to combat electronic penetrations, data thefts, and cyberattacks on critical information systems. CCIPS prevents, investigates, and prosecutes computer crimes by working with other government agencies, the private sector, academic institutions, and foreign counterparts."

CCIPS lawyers assist in complicated investigations, addressing the legal issues that are involved. Later, they try cases or support prosecuting attorneys. They also help train law enforcement workers (federal, state, and local). They provide input on new laws related to cyber crime and cooperate with international agencies.

JOBS IN THE PRIVATE SECTOR

Employers include countless large businesses and corporations of every type—all who rely heavily on the Internet and recognize the need for secure operations. Prospective employees must usually have the computer-related degrees and skills described earlier. Specific duties vary, though, depending on the employer's use of information technology and the Net. In some workplaces, advancement opportunities abound. In others, the needs are limited and so are promotion prospects.

New programmers are usually placed under the supervision of experienced programmers. They are given such assignments as writing simple computer programs and updating the code in existing programs. When they are ready, they are given important programming assignments to develop on their own. "They then advance to more difficult programming assignments, and may become project supervisors," the *Occupational Outlook Handbook* explains. "With continued experience, they may move into management positions within their organizations. Some programmers advance into software engineering positions, and others become systems analysts."

Systems analysts generally start with limited responsibilities. They may begin working with experienced analysts or may deal with small systems or with one aspect of a larger system. As they gain experience and further their education, they may move into supervisory or management positions. Systems analysts who work with one type of system, or one aspect or application of a system, may become specialty consultants.

Software engineers who show leadership ability can become project managers or advance into management

These young hackers in South Korea in 2009 compete in an exercise to demonstrate how infiltrators took down numerous Web sites in their country and the United States.

positions, such as manager of information systems or chief information officer. Computer support specialists can advance by becoming experts in an area that leads to other opportunities. For example, those responsible for network support might advance into network administration or network security positions.

OUTSIDE CONTRACTORS

Many security specialists don't work directly for government agencies or private companies. Rather, they work for service companies that contract with agencies and corporations

USING THE INTERNET TO FIND A NET JOB

Not surprisingly, Internet security students and professionals take advantage of the Internet itself to search for career opportunities and advancement. Online job hunting takes several forms. Simply Googling search terms such as "computer courses," "Internet security jobs," or "cyber security careers" will lead to training programs, job banks specializing in technology employment, articles and other background material for career seekers, and actual job openings.

The most effective job searches, however, may be the ones that take advantage of what the Internet does best: networking. Michael Farr, author of *Top 100 Computer and Technical Careers*, says, "The fact is that most jobs are not advertised, so how do you find them? The same way that about two-thirds of all job seekers do: networking with people you know (which I call making warm contacts) and directly contacting employers (which I call making cold contacts)."

Phil Bartlett, writing in the *Computer Science Résumés and Job-Finding Guide*, discusses the advantages and disadvantages of using online job-posting services and of posting résumés online. Online job posting is fast and convenient, he notes, and can provide "wider exposure to a variety of jobs than other methods." It can be frustrating, though, because hundreds of candidates may apply for one job. That means most applications are virtually buried.

to handle IT matters, including security. Service company employees may work almost entirely inside their service company's offices. On the other hand, they may spend much of their time onsite, at a client company that engages their services.

The *Occupational Outlook Handbook* describes how the growing use of networks—Internet and intranets—calls for greater information security. Many organizations, the handbook acknowledges, turn to outside consulting firms that specialize in IT security. "These firms assess computer systems for areas of vulnerability, manage firewalls, and provide protection against intrusion and software 'viruses.'"

Many professionals in this field are so skilled and Internet-experienced that they are able to resolve certain problems online from wherever they happen to be. Powerful computers equipped with special software and with access to online resources are their tools. In some cases, they can go into a client's system, locate the point of hacker attack, and remedy the situation—from hundreds or thousands of miles away.

The *Occupational Outlook Handbook* points out that "given the technology available today . . . more work can be done from remote locations using e-mail and the Internet. For example, systems analysts may work from home with their computers linked directly to computers at the location of their employer or client. Computer support specialists, likewise, can tap into a customer's computer remotely in order to identify and fix problems. Even programmers and consultants, who often relocate to a customer's place of business while working on a project, may perform work from offsite locations."

Some contracting firms focus entirely on the security aspect of information technology. Others offer teams of professionals who can handle all areas of a client's information technology needs. Outside IT professionals design, install, and maintain information systems for various organizations. They make sure the organizations' data are protected by firewalls and other tools. In some cases, their programmers write security software specifically for the client organization. They develop a disaster recovery plan and help the organization return to work quickly in the event of a computer breakdown, natural disaster, or security breach.

PREPARE AN EFFECTIVE RÉSUMÉ

A high school student—even one who has no job or experience in any career category—should create a career résumé. A résumé is a record of a person's work history and personal background that might affect job performance. It tells prospective employers about the applicant's Internet technology skills and any other skills and experience. It also contains information about the individual's career objectives, educational background, personal interests, and special accomplishments and awards.

The person's name, address, phone number, and e-mail address are stated at the top of the résumé; many résumé builders also include a photograph of themselves. At the end are the names and contact details of several references—people who will vouch for the applicant's character and capabilities. (References may be included only if they give their permission.) Workers should update their résumés often, as they acquire new skills, experience, and training.

Individuals who have no work experience can prepare what is called a functional résumé. It simply states the person's career goals, personal interests, and educational record.

A chronological résumé will be appropriate after the person gains experience on the job. It describes each job the person has held (including those unrelated to the Internet or technology), beginning with the current or most recent employment. Each job description should mention specific responsibilities the worker held, software and hardware that was mastered and used on the job, and the reason for leaving.

When applying for a job in person, by e-mail, or by letter, the person will give the interviewer a copy of the résumé to examine and place on file. When applying by letter or e-mail, the résumé should be accompanied by a short cover letter. A cover letter should be crafted to attract the employer's attention immediately, pointing to special qualifications the applicant has. It should express the applicant's sincere interest not just in general employment, but in that particular job and employer.

A REWARDING CAREER

A career in Internet security will be rewarding in many ways. Primarily, it is a tremendous service to modern society. It is challenging, exciting work. It also pays well, in most situations.

Internet security workers rarely suffer physical injuries, except those common to most computer-related careers: eye strain from the screen and repetitive motion ailments such as carpal tunnel syndrome from constant keyboarding.

However, it is not a "cushy" job that involves easy hours with few demands. People who work with computer systems and in related jobs average almost thirty-nine-hour workweeks—five hours more than the average in other industries—according to the *Occupational Outlook Handbook*. Information security specialists must stay on top of the security operations of their employers and clients. They may have to respond to highly stressful emergencies at any hour of the day or night.

CHAPTER 6

Future Demands in Internet Security

Computer security executives are alarmed. A 2009 survey indicated most of them believe modern society's communication and energy systems face mounting threats via the Internet. Most fear their firms will be affected by a major attack in the next few years; many have already been attacked.

The international study was made by the Center for Strategic and International Studies, a research firm, working with security software maker McAfee. Two out of five survey participants anticipated a major breach in the next year; about 80 percent expected one in the next five years. A "major incident" was defined as one resulting in a loss of operations for twenty-four hours or longer, failure of the victimized company, or loss of life.

Individual PCs, as well as corporate computer systems, are at risk. In one incident, hackers stole the ID of a corporation president and used it in an international drug ring. He found out about it when drug enforcement officers roused him from bed at gunpoint one morning. Hackers sometimes boldly attack the very professionals who combat them. By breaking into a health care database, for instance, criminals obtained the information needed to access the checking account of a U.S. prosecutor. The irony was that the prosecutor had earned a reputation for convicting ID thieves.

Concerns became more worrying in 2009. Two separate onslaughts of cyber attacks on U.S. companies were traced to

The National Security Agency and other government offices maintain career sections on their Web sites. Interested young people can find information about educational requirements and available jobs.

sources in China. Technology observers wondered whether the hackers were connected with the Chinese government. Similar Internet problems have been traced for years to countries known to be at odds with the United States. Security specialists can usually trace the origin of attack to a country but cannot prove it was the work of a government agency or a hacker who might be in the agency's employ.

Because of the nature of their operations, national security agencies like the FBI, Secret Service, and Department of Homeland Security do not publish statistics on Internet crime cases. By all accounts, though, the numbers of investigations and arrests are on the increase.

GOOD NEWS FOR CAREER HUNTERS

Pessimism and alarm among system managers translates to optimism and excitement for people interested in Internet security careers. One sign is that the National Security Agency lists computer scientists among the "hot jobs" in its online careers section. Christopher Drew, in a 2009 *New York Times* article about the need for more information security professionals, points out that "as attacks on vital computer systems proliferate, surveys show a serious shortage of talent to combat them. Banks, military contractors, and software companies, along with federal agencies, are looking for 'cyber ninjas' to fend off a sophisticated array of hackers, from criminals stealing credit card numbers to potential military adversaries."

Every day, the body of information contained on the Internet grows. The number of possible connections between people and resources expands our ability to communicate. All of this makes the Net increasingly important in the lives of twenty-first-century citizens. It also makes it an irresistible target for people who use the Internet for evil purposes— stealing information, stealing other people's identities, and destroying the lives of innocent Internet users.

Mark Weatherford, chief information security officer for the state of California, observes that most criminals "congregate where the money is." He states ominously, "Cyber criminals are no different, and as long as the barriers to entry remain low (they are) and the risk of getting caught is almost zero (it is), cyber crime is going to blossom. While the on-line economy grows, so do the cyber crime opportunities." He predicts "continued growth in crime and the exploitation of people through social media technologies that allow cyber criminals to prey not only on the naïve, but all of us by means of credit card fraud, phishing, identity theft, and distribu-tion of child pornography."

For those reasons, Weatherford believes organizations are beginning to recruit and train more cyber security experts. He points to a "shrinking pool of technical cyber security talent" within security organizations. Hackers are becoming more sophisticated in what they do. Organizations that don't keep pace by employing skilled security workers, he says, can-not protect themselves.

Weatherford cites reports that the supply of Internet security and IT expert talent is lagging behind the need to confront hacker threats. "In the public sector where I work, the 'retirement bubble' we've been hearing about for a couple of years now is becoming very real and we need to begin grow-ing the next generation of cyber security experts now."

NOTABLE CAREER FIELDS

The U.S. Bureau of Labor Statistics' *Occupational Outlook Handbook, 2010–11 Edition*, projects computer system design and its related services to be among the ten fastest-growing career fields in the United States. Computer specialists should have the most promising opportunities within that category.

Growth is also expected in computer system security jobs. "Security specialists will be employed more often to assess a

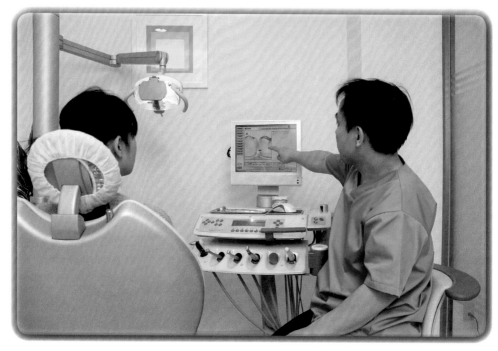

Offices and institutions worldwide, ranging from medical practices to banks to educational facilities, rely heavily on computer technology. This trend creates greater demand for security professionals.

system's vulnerability and implement security measures. In addition, analysts and developers will be needed to develop new antivirus software, programs, and procedures." That bodes well for future systems analysts, software engineers, and consultants, especially those involved in disaster recovery, specialized programming, and IT systems security.

In general, the growth of computer technology and Internet use will create new jobs not just in security but also in related areas. Networking specialists and system integrators— people who make hardware, software, and communications function together effectively—will be in demand. Wireless technology in its different forms calls for new services and product specialists. Wireless devices have given people greater networking mobility, whether they are on the job or at their leisure. Some users almost always are online. This new lifestyle among individuals and within businesses creates "an increased need for professionals that can design and integrate computer systems so that they will be compatible with mobile technologies," according to the *Occupational Outlook Handbook*.

In addition to the employment prospects discussed above and in previous chapters, young people may want to look for unique job scenarios. The handbook points to health care as an example of an industry that is expected to intensify its use of information technology. Patients today can order prescriptions online and obtain health records in electronic formats. This means secure information technology platforms are essential in hospitals, doctors' offices, and related health care facilities.

Jobs in finance-related security will obviously expand. The Federal Trade Commission and various financial agencies are required to monitor transactions of bank and credit card accounts. This helps them detect patterns of withdrawals that may suggest ID theft or patterns of deposits that could point to other illegal activities. Increased credit card transactions in recent decades have presented a need for more security professionals in this area.

Security experts who address issues in cloud computing may be in special demand in the future. Dan Kaminsky, network security specialist for IOActive, a computer security service, predicts: "The Cloud is going to win. . . . It's faster. It's better. It's cheaper. But there are security issues. . . . Genuine, technical security faults in cloud technology will garner a huge amount of attention."

THE PRICE OF INSECURITY CAN BE STEEP

Companies and organizations that fail to secure their computer systems and electronic information risk grave problems for themselves, their employees, and others whose confidential information they keep. They also face heavy government fines and other punishment.

The Federal Trade Commission (FTC) recently fined a company $275,000 because its security and monitoring system failed to prevent a hacker from obtaining consumers' personal information. In addition, the FTC required a government review of the company's security practices every two years for the next twenty years.

In another case, the FTC fined a children's apparel company $250,000. The company reportedly had collected personal information about child customers online without obtaining permission from or notifying the parents.

To cope with rising computer crimes, legislatures and government agencies are requiring stricter corporate security policies. Every company that collects personal information over the Internet needs technical and legal experts who understand the requirements and can make sure they are obeyed. Some companies hire their own staff professionals in these areas. Others contract with outside support services.

Federal and state legislatures are trying to bolster Internet security by passing new laws that require organizations to protect information and individual privacy. A key example is the Health Insurance Portability and Accountability Act (HIPAA). Its regulations impose stronger requirements for companies and organizations to secure individuals' health information. As new data protection and Internet security laws are passed, more trained professionals will be needed to make sure the requirements are met.

Security services and product providers are coming up with new ways to protect their clients' electronic information. An example is 3BView, an international technology company that specializes in removing metadata from documents for law firms, corporations, and government agencies. Metadata include hidden information about a data file, such as changes that have been made to it by different people. Metadata details can be very sensitive. For that reason, courts and government agencies regulate the security of metadata. With the increased use of Webmail and mobile devices like BlackBerries, iPhones, and netbooks to exchange documents, the problem has grown. 3BView's engineers have developed a way to remove metadata from files sent from such mobile devices. This helps the senders ensure that they follow the rules.

A DIVERSE CAREER FIELD

Whether the task is to develop new IT tools and techniques, ensure the security of a network, enforce laws, or actively pursue cyber criminals, Internet security involves a wide array of careers. The *Occupational Outlook Handbook* concludes that "as individuals and organizations continue to conduct business electronically, the importance of maintaining system and network security will increase. Employment opportunities should be especially good for individuals involved in cyberspace security services, such as disaster recovery services, custom security programming, and security software installation services."

More jobs in the Internet security field will open up as government agencies, financial institutions, computer firms, and other key players recognize the intensity of the so-called cyber war. FBI director Robert Mueller has acknowledged that despite all the agency's efforts, "we are still outnumbered by cyber criminals." He adds, "We all have a responsibility to protect the infrastructure that protects the world."

Glossary

blog (Weblog) A Web location where the owner (and friends, if allowed) posts opinions, notes, and information; blogs have been called digital diaries.

botnet Short for "robot" and "network," a botnet is a network of computers on which malicious software has been installed by worms or other malware. It allows a "master" computer to control the network remotely.

code The language with which a software program gives digital instructions to a computer.

confidential information Private information that one person shares with another, with the understanding that it is not to be passed on to anyone else.

cryptography In computer science, the encoding and decoding of data.

database A body of related information stored on a computer.

defragmentation The technical process of consolidating chunks of related data on a computer disk to improve data access speed.

diagnostic utility A computer program designed to locate and correct specific types of problems in a computer system.

encryption The conversion of text into coded form so that only authorized people can read it.

extranet An intranet that is partly accessible to authorized outsiders, who have a valid user name and password; the outsider's identity distinguishes what parts of the extranet the person can view.

firewall A software or hardware "electronic wall" designed to block hacker attacks.

help desk An office or department that solves computer problems and offers technical advice.

hyperlink A link on a Web page or in a digital document that instantly takes the reader to another location.

information technology (IT) Computerized information and communications and the management of them.

infrastructure The underlying foundation of a system; the large-scale public systems, services, and facilities of a country or region that are necessary for economic activity, including water and power supplies, public transportation, telecommunications, roads, and schools.

intellectual property Works that come under copyright or trademark protection.

interface The system by which a person interacts with a computer or the Internet.

intranet An Internet-like network belonging to an organization or business that is accessible only by that group's employees or people with authorization and that is protected by a firewall.

malicious Evil-intentioned, spiteful, or mean.

malware Any mischievous, harmful, or intrusive type of software, including viruses, worms, spyware, and other programs.

metadata, metatag Unseen programming information that labels or describes visible information.

password A combination of letters and/or numbers used by an individual to log onto restricted programs or Internet locations.

phishing An attempt to steal an Internet user's account information by luring the user to a bogus bank or credit card site.

protocol In computing and Internet usage, a set of programming rules that determine how data are formatted and treated.

social networking Using the Internet to establish a personal network of contacts, or virtual community.

utility program A program designed to make a computer more efficient, rather than to provide applications for the end user.

Web 2.0 The concept of making the World Wide Web more of an interactive community of users.

Webmail E-mail transmitted, usually free, by a popular Internet entity such as Google or AOL, not by a paid local e-mail service provider.

For More Information

Bureau of Labor Statistics (BLS)
U.S. Department of Labor
2 Massachusetts Avenue NE, Suite 2135
Washington, DC 20212-0001
(202) 691-5700
Web site: http://www.bls.gov
The BLS updates the *Occupational Outlook Handbook,* which
describes thousands of careers with details about job
requirements and average salaries.

Computer Crime and Intellectual Property Section (CCIPS)
U.S. Department of Justice
10th Street and Constitution Avenue NW
John C. Keeney Building, Suite 600
Washington, DC 20530
(202) 514-1026
Web site: http://www.justice.gov/criminal/cybercrime/cc.html
The CCIPS is "responsible for implementing the depart-
ment's national strategies in combating computer and
intellectual property crimes worldwide."

Federal Bureau of Investigation (FBI)
J. Edgar Hoover Building
935 Pennsylvania Avenue NW
Washington, DC 20535-0001
(202) 324-3000
Web site: http://www.fbi.gov

Among its varied other work, the FBI thwarts computer
   intrusions, identifies and apprehends online sexual
   predators, and counteracts national and transnational
   organized crime on the Internet.

Human Resources and Skills Development Canada
Ottawa, ON K1A OJ2
Canada
(819) 994-5559
Web site: http://www.hrsdc.gc.ca/eng/labour/index.shtml
This organization provides information about job openings
   in Canada.

ISC2 Americas
1964 Gallows Road, Suite 210
Vienna, VA 22182
(866) 462-4777, (703) 891-6781
Web site: http://www.isc2.org
The International Information Systems Security Certification
   Consortium, Inc., is a nonprofit organization that
   offers training and certification programs for security
   professionals.

SANS Technology Institute
8120 Woodmont Avenue, Suite 205
Bethesda, MD 20814
(301) 654-7267
Web site: http://www.sans.org
The institute offers computer security training as well as
   resource material. Courses are taught online and onsite.

U.S. Computer Emergency Readiness Team (US-CERT)
U.S. Department of Homeland Security
245 Murray Lane SW, Building 410
Washington, DC 20598
(888) 282-0870
Web site: http://www.us-cert.gov
This branch of the Department of Homeland Security provides support and defense against cyber attacks for the
federal government.

U.S. Department of Homeland Security
Washington, DC 29528
(202) 282-8000
Web site: http://www.dhs.gov
The Department of Homeland Security is one of several fed-
eral agencies that employ cyber security specialists.

WEB SITES

Due to the changing nature of Internet links, Rosen
Publishing has developed an online list of Web sites related
to the subject of this book. This site is updated regularly.
Please use this link to access the list:

http://www.rosenlinks.com/cict/ciis

Bailey, Diane. *Cyber Ethics* (Cyber Citizenship and
    Cyber Safety). New York, NY: Rosen Publishing
    Group, 2008.

Bartlett, Phil J. *Computer Science Résumés and Job-Finding
    Guide.* Hauppauge, NY: Barron's Educational Series,
    Inc., 2005.

Byers, Ann. *Great Résumé, Application, and Interview Skills*
    (Work Readiness). New York, NY: Rosen Publishing
    Group, 2008.

Day-MacLeod, Deirdre. *Viruses and Spam* (Cyber Citizenship
    and Cyber Safety). New York, NY: Rosen Publishing
    Group, 2008.

Farr, Michael. *Top 100 Computer and Technical Careers.* 4th ed.
    Indianapolis, IN: JIST Publishing, 2009.

Ferguson's Careers in Focus: Computers. 5th ed. New York, NY:
    Facts on File, 2008.

Gookin, Dan. *Troubleshooting Your PC for Dummies.* 3rd ed.
    Hoboken, NJ: Wiley Publishing, Inc., 2008.

Gray, Leon. *Virtual Crime: Solving Cybercrime* (Solve That
    Crime!). Berkeley Heights, NJ: Enslow Publishers, 2009.

McCoy, Lisa. *Computers and Programming* (Career Launcher).
    New York, NY: Facts on File, 2010.

Orr, Tamra B. *Privacy and Hacking* (Cyber Citizenship and Cyber
    Safety). New York, NY: Rosen Publishing Group, 2008.

Reeves, Diane Lindsey. *Career Ideas for Teens in Information
    Technology* (Career Ideas for Teens). New York, NY:
    Chelsea House Publishers, 2005.

Bell, Gavin. *Building Social Networking Applications.* Sebastopol, CA: O'Reilly Media, Inc., 2009.

Bender, David. "Data Breaches in the Cloud: Looks Like Rain?" *New York Law Journal,* August 5, 2009. Retrieved January 2010 (http://www.law.com/jsp/lawtechnologynews/PubArticleLTN.jsp?id=1202432771872&Data_Breaches_in_the_Cloud_Looks_Like_Rain).

Brenner, Bill. "10 Predictions for 2010: Kaminsky and Weatherford." Threat Post: The Kaspersky Lab Security News Service, December 14, 2009. Retrieved January 2010 (http://threatpost.com).

Buckley, Peter, and Duncan Clark. *The Rough Guide to the Internet.* 11th ed. New York, NY: Rough Guides/Penguin Putnam, Inc., 2005.

Bureau of Labor Statistics, U.S. Department of Labor. "Computer Systems Design and Related Services." *Occupational Outlook Handbook, 2010–11.* Retrieved December 28, 2009 (http://www.bls.gov/oco/cg/CGS033.htm#related).

Bureau of Labor Statistics, U.S. Department of Labor. "Telecommunications." *Career Guide to Industries, 2010–11.* Retrieved January 2010 (http://www.bls.gov/oco/cg/CGS020.htm).

CBS News. "Do Clues Point to Global Hack Conspiracy?" January 13, 2010. Retrieved January 27, 2010 (http://www.cbsnews.com/stories/2010/01/13/tech/cnettechnews/main602375.shtml).

Downing, Douglas A., et al. *Dictionary of Computer and Internet Terms.* 10th ed. Hauppauge, NY: Barron's Educational Series, Inc., 2009.

Drew, Christopher. "Wanted: Cyber Ninjas." *New York Times,* December 29, 2009. Retrieved January 2010 (http://www.nytimes.com/2010/01/03/education/edlife/03cybersecurity.html).

Federal Bureau of Investigation. "Operation Phish Phry: Major Cyber Fraud Takedown." October 7, 2009. Retrieved January 2010 (http://www.fbi.gov/page2/oct09/phishphry_100709.html).

Georgia Tech College of Computing. "Georgia Tech Creates New Online Master's Degree in Information Security." November 16, 2009. Retrieved February 9, 2010 (http://www.cc.gatech.edu/news/georgia-tech-creates-new-online-masters-degree-in-information-security).

Goodstein, Anastasia. *Totally Wired: What Teens and Tweens Are Really Doing Online.* New York, NY: St. Martin's Griffin, 2007.

Gross, Dan. "Experts: U.S. Gov't Needs to Prepare for Cyberwar." *PCWorld*/IDG News Service, January 27, 2010. Retrieved January 31, 2010 (http://www.pcworld.com/article/187952/experts_us_govt_needs_to_prepare_for_cyberwar.html).

Harmon, Daniel E. "Unfriendly Connections: Online Networking Is Cool . . . But It Has Its Risks." *The Lawyer's PC,* July 1, 2009, pp. 1–5.

Infosecurity.com. "Healthcare Hacks on the Rise." January 26, 2010. Retrieved January 27, 2010 (http://www.infosecurity-us.com/view/6806/healthcare-hacks-on-the-rise).

Krebs on Security. "Texas Banks Sues Customer Hit by $800,000 Cyber Heist." January 26, 2010. Retrieved January 27, 2010 (http://www.krebsonsecurity.com/2010/01/texas-bank-sues-customer-hit-by-800000-cyber-heist).

Markoff, John. "Survey of Executives Finds a Growing Fear of Cyberattacks." *New York Times*, January 28, 2010. Retrieved January 29, 2010 (http://www/nytimes.com/2010/01/29/science/29cyber.html?ref=technology).

Markoff, John, and Ashlee Vance. "Fearing Hackers Who Leave No Trace." *New York Times*, January 20, 2010. Retrieved January 20, 2010 (http://www.nytimes.com/2010/01/20/technology/20code.html).

Mitic, Scott. *Stopping Identity Theft: 10 Easy Steps to Security*. Berkeley, CA: Nolo/USA Today, 2009.

Rhoads, C. J. *The Entrepreneur's Guide to Managing Information Technology*. Westport, CT: Praeger Publishers, 2008.

Skandier, Toby. *Network Administrator Street Smarts: A Real World Guide to CompTIA Network+ Skills*. 2nd ed. Hoboken, NJ: Wiley Publishing, Inc., 2009.

Stein, Richard Joseph, ed. *Internet Security*. New York, NY: The H. W. Wilson Company, 2009.

Threat Post: The Kaspersky Lab Security News Service. "Tough Road Ahead for Adobe on Security." January 8, 2010. Retrieved January 27, 2010 (http://threatpost.com/en_us/blogs/tough-road-ahead-adobe-security-010810?utm_source=Threatpost+Spotlight+Email&utm_medium=Email+Marketing+-+CRM+List&utm_campaign=Threatpost+Spotlight&CID=).

3BView. "3BView Announces Launch of 3BCleanDocs via SaaS." Press release, December 3, 2009 (http://www.3bview.com).

U.S. Department of Justice. "Alleged International Hacking Ring Caught in $9 Million Fraud." November 10, 2009. Retrieved January 2010 (http://www.justice.gov/opa/pr/2009/November/09-crm-1212.html).

Weinberg, Neal. "Cloud Computing: Hot Technology for 2009." *Network World*, January 5, 2009. Retrieved February 9, 2010 (http://www.networkworld.com/supp/2009/outlook/hottech/010509-nine-hot-techs-cloud-computing.html).

Weisman, Steve. *50 Ways to Protect Your Identity and Your Credit.* Upper Saddle River, NJ: Pearson Education, Inc./Prentice Hall, 2005.

White, Ron. *How Computers Work.* 8th ed. Indianapolis, IN: QUE Publishing, 2006.

Willison, Simon. "Web Security Horror Stories: The Director's Cut." Weblog presentation, October 26, 2008. Retrieved January 2010 (http://simonwillison.net/2008/talks/head-horror).

Index

ABOUT THE AUTHOR

Daniel E. Harmon is the author of more than seventy books and thousands of magazine, newspaper, and newsletter articles. He is the longtime editor/author of *The Lawyer's PC,* a national technology newsletter for legal professionals. His computer- and Internet-related articles have appeared in numerous technology periodicals. Harmon's previous career books include *Electrician, Careers in the Corrections System, Careers in Explosives and Arson Investigation,* and *Jobs in Environmental Cleanup and Emergency Hazmat Response.* He lives in Spartanburg, South Carolina.

PHOTO CREDITS

Cover (background, front and back), p. 1 (top left, background) © www.istockphoto.com/Audrey Prokhorov; cover (front inset), p. 9 Shutterstock; chapter art © www.istockphoto.com/ Daniel Brunner; interior backgrounds © www.istockphoto.com/ Nicholas Belton; pp. 7, 26, 42, 43, 50, 53 © AP Images; p. 15 Joe Raedle/ Getty Images; p. 19 © Newscom; p. 22 © www.istockphoto.com/Krzystof Zmij; p. 28 © Symantec Corp.; p. 33 © www.istockphoto.com; p. 36 © www.istockphoto.com/Jacob Wackerhausen; p. 38 © Flirt/SuperStock; p. 62 Martin Holtkamp/Taxi Japan/Getty Images.

Designer: Matthew Cauli; Editor: Kathy Kuhtz Campbell; Photo Researcher: Marty Levick